Table of Contents

8

Disclaimers

The information provided herein is intended to provide general information and entertainment purposes only. Use of the information in this book is at your own risk.

The author does not assume any responsibility for any personal injury or damage to property that may occur as a result of reading this book.

The information in this book is believed to be accurate as of the date it was published, but no warranty is made regarding its accuracy or completeness. The author and publisher disclaim any liability in connection with the use of this information.

This book is not intended to be a substitute for professional tax, accounting, financial, investment, legal, or medical advice.

This book is not a substitute for professional tax or accounting advice. Readers should consult a qualified accountant for specific advice.

This book is not a substitute for professional financial or investment advice. Readers should consult a qualified financial advisor for specific advice. There is a risk of loss in any investment. Results are not typical and will vary from person to person. You may not make any money at all. In fact, you could lose money. No specific investment recommendations are made. The book does not take into account the reader's investment objectives, financial situation, or needs. Before making any investment decisions, readers are advised to consult with their financial advisor.

This book is not a substitute for professional legal advice. Readers should consult a qualified licensed attorney in your jurisdiction for specific advice. This book does not create an attorney-client relationship between you and the author.

This book is not a substitute for professional medical advice. Readers should consult a qualified healthcare professional for specific advice. You should always consult with a licensed healthcare professional in your jurisdiction before making any medical decisions. This book does not create a physician-patient relationship between you and the author.

Introduction

How can artificial intelligence be used to create machines that think and behave like humans? This question has long intrigued scientists and researchers in the field of AI. And it is a question that this book will attempt to answer.

By developing artificial neural networks, training them to recognize human facial expressions, and making machine learning algorithms that can identify objects, faces, and scenes like humans, we can begin to create AI systems that think and learn in similar ways to humans. In addition, by observing how humans learn, we can develop predictive models of human behavior that human interactions can use to guide machine learning. And by studying how people use natural language, we can create AI systems that can interact with humans in more natural ways.

This book will explore all of these topics in greater detail, providing readers with a better understanding of how AI can be used to create machines that think and behave like humans. In doing so, we will examine some ethical and legal issues associated with using AI technologies.

Creating neural networks that simulate the workings of the human brain

Neural networks are a powerful tool for artificial intelligence, allowing machines to learn and make decisions in a way that is similar to humans. However, current neural networks are limited in their ability to simulate the workings of the human brain.

One way to overcome this limitation is to create neural networks that are more closely based on the structure of the human brain. This would involve creating networks with more layers, neurons, and connections between neurons.

Another way to improve the ability of neural networks to simulate the human brain is to use different types of neurons. Most neural networks use artificial neurons based on real neurons' structures. However, there are many kinds of neurons in the human brain, each with its unique function.

By using different types of neurons, it may be possible to create neural networks that more accurately simulate the workings of the human brain.

In addition to using different types of neurons, it is also essential to use the right connections between neurons. Current neural networks typically use fully connected layers, where every neuron is connected to every other neuron in the next layer.

However, the human brain uses a much more efficient type of connection called sparse connections. Only a tiny fraction of neurons are connected in sparsely connected neural networks.

By using sparsely connected layers, it is possible to create neural networks that are much more efficient and closer to the structure of the human brain.

There are many other ways to improve the ability of neural networks to simulate the workings of the human brain. For example, it is essential to use the correct type of activation function. Currently, most neural networks use linear activation functions, but the human brain uses non-linear activation functions.

By using non-linear activation functions, it is possible to create neural networks more similar to the workings of the human brain.

Many other design choices can be made to improve the ability of neural networks to simulate the workings of the human brain. However, these are just a few of the most important design choices that need to be made.

By developing artificial neural networks

By developing artificial neural networks inspired by how the human brain works, we can create machines that can think more like humans. This could potentially lead to a future where devices can help us solve problems that we may not be able to solve on our own.

One way that artificial neural networks can be used to create machines that think like humans are by providing them with a similar kind of input. For example, if we were to provide an artificial neural network with images of different objects, we would be able to learn about the different shapes and sizes of those objects. Similarly, if we were to provide an artificial neural network with spoken words, we would be able to learn about the different sounds that make up those words.

Another way that artificial neural networks can be used to create machines that think like humans are by providing them with a similar kind of output. For example, if we were to provide an artificial neural network with a list of items, it would be able to generate a sentence that describes those items. Similarly, if we were to provide an artificial neural network with a set of instructions, it would be able to generate a set of actions that accomplishes those instructions.

By providing artificial neural networks with both input and output similar to how humans process information, we can create machines that are much better at thinking like humans. This could potentially lead to a future where devices can help us solve problems that we may not be able to solve on our own.

Training artificial neural networks to recognize human facial expressions

Most machine learning algorithms used today are based on a branch of mathematics called statistics. Statisticians have developed robust methods for analyzing data that can be used to find patterns and trends. However, these methods are not well suited for analyzing data that is complex or non-linear, such as images or video.

Neural networks are a type of machine learning algorithm that is well suited for analyzing complex data. Neural networks are similar to the brain in that they are composed of many interconnected processing nodes or neurons. Each neuron receives input from many other neurons and produces an output passed to other neurons.

Neural networks are trained by presenting them with examples of the data they are supposed to learn. For example, if we want to train a neural network to recognize human faces, we would show it many pictures of faces, along with the labels (e.g., "male," "female," "child," etc.). The neural network would then learn to associate specific patterns of pixel values with the labels.

Once a neural network has been trained, it can be used to make predictions about new data. For example, if we showed the face-recognition neural network a picture of a person it had never seen before, it would attempt to label that person based on the patterns it had learned.

There are many different types of neural networks, and each type is well suited for solving another kind of problem. This blog post will focus on convolutional neural networks (CNNs), which are particularly well-suitable for image recognition tasks.

Making machine learning algorithms that can identify objects, faces, and scenes like humans

In recent years, there has been an explosion of interest in artificial intelligence (AI). A primary focus of AI research is to develop algorithms that can identify objects, faces, and scenes in digital images, just like humans can.

Convolutional neural networks (CNNs) are a machine learning algorithm that has succeeded in this task. CNN's are inspired by the structure of the visual cortex, the part of the brain that processes visual information.

One of the critical features of CNNs is that they learn to extract increasingly abstract and higher-level representations of the data as they are trained. For example, a CNN might start by learning to detect simple edge patterns in images. Then, as it is trained on more data, it might learn to see more complex designs, such as shapes or faces.

This process of learning increasingly abstract representations is similar to how humans learn to recognize objects. For example, when a baby sees a toy for the first time, they don't immediately recognize it as a toy. But after seeing many different toys, they learn to generalize and recognize all toys as belonging to the same category.

One of the challenges in training CNNs is that they require a large amount of data to learn from. This is where humans have an advantage over machines: we are exposed to billions of images from a young age, which gives us a vast amount of data to learn from.

Another challenge is that CNNs are very good at recognizing objects in well-lit images with clear boundaries. But they often struggle with more challenging scenarios, such as identifying objects partially hidden or obscured by other objects.

One way to overcome these challenges is to use Generative Adversarial Networks (GANs). GANs are neural networks that can generate realistic images from scratch. They are composed of two parts: a generator and discriminator networks.

The generator network takes as input a noise vector and generates an image from it. The discriminator network then tries to distinguish between real and fake images generated by the generator network.

As the generator and discriminator networks are trained together, they get better at their respective tasks. For example, the generator network learns to generate realistic images, while the discriminator network learns to distinguish between real and fake photos better.

GANs have been used to generate realistic images of faces, scenes, and objects. They can also create pictures from textual descriptions, such as "a man riding a horse."

One advantage of using GANs is that they can be trained on small amounts of data. This is because the generator network can learn to generate realistic images even if it has only seen a few real examples.

Another advantage of GANs is that they can help CNNs learn to recognize objects better in challenging scenarios. For example, if we train a GAN to generate realistic images of faces from scratch, it will learn to create looks that are well-lit and have clear boundaries. But it will also learn to create faces that are partially hidden or obscured.

Investigating how humans learn to create AI systems that can learn in similar ways

It is widely accepted that developing artificial intelligence (AI) systems that can learn similarly to humans is critical to achieving true AI. After all, humans are the current gold standard for learning ability, so it stands to reason that if we can create machines that can learn like us, they will be much more intelligent than they are now.

There are many ways humans learn, so there is no one-size-fits-all approach to creating AI systems that can learn like us. However, there are some commonalities between how humans learn and how AI systems currently learn that can be exploited to create more human-like AI.

One of the most critical aspects of human learning is our ability to learn from very few examples. This is known as one-shot learning, which current AI systems struggle with. For example, if you show a child a picture of a cat and tell them it is a cat, they will be able to immediately recognize other pictures of cats as being cats, even if they have never seen that particular cat before. However, if you show an AI system a cat picture and tell it that it is a cat, it will only be able to recognize other pictures of cats if it has seen many different cats beforehand.

One reason why one-shot learning is so difficult for AI systems is that they rely on statistical methods to learn, and these methods are not well suited to one-shot learning. Another reason is that AI systems do not have the same kind of general intelligence that humans have, so they cannot make the same kinds of inferences from limited data that we can.

However, there has been some recent progress on one-shot learning in AI, which may lead to more human-like AI. For example, researchers have developed an AI system that can learn from just one example using a memory-based approach instead of a statistical approach. This could be used to create AI systems that can learn new concepts from just a few examples, in much the same way humans do.

In addition to one-shot learning, another important aspect of human understanding is our ability to transfer knowledge from one context to another. This is known as transfer learning, which current AI systems are not very good at. For example, if you learn how to drive a car in the UK, you will be able to drive a vehicle in any other country with little difficulty. However, if you train an AI system to drive a car in the UK, it will not be able to drive a vehicle in any other country unless it has been specifically trained.

Transfer learning is so difficult for AI systems because they tend to overfit the training data. That is, they learn the specific details of the training data too well and cannot generalize this knowledge to other data sets. On the other hand, humans are very good at transfer learning because we have evolved to deal with changing environments.

Building predictive models of human behavior based on data mining and machine learning techniques

When it comes to artificial intelligence, one of the key goals is to create machines that can think like humans. After all, if we can build machines that think and learn as we do, they will be much more powerful and valuable than current AI technology.

There are many ways to create machines that think like humans. One approach is to build predictive models of human behavior based on data mining and machine learning techniques. This approach has been quite successful recently, with many companies and organizations using it significantly.

The key to this approach is to collect as much data as possible on human behavior. This data can come from various sources, including social media, online activity, surveys, etc. Once you have a large dataset, you can use machine learning algorithms to find patterns and trends in the data.

You can then build predictive models of human behavior based on these patterns. These models can be used to make predictions about what people will do in the future and can also be used to help make decisions about how to interact with people.

This approach has several advantages. First, it can be very accurate. If you have a large enough dataset, you can usually find precise patterns in the data. Second, it is relatively easy to implement. Many different machine learning algorithms can be used for this purpose, and many different ways to collect data.

Third, this approach can predict a wide range of human behaviors. For example, you could use it to predict what products people will buy, their actions on social media, or even how they will vote in an election. Fourth, predictive models can be updated relatively quickly as new data becomes available.

Finally, predictive models can be used in many different ways. For example, they can be used to personalize content or advertisements that are shown to people. They can also be used to help automate decision-making processes.

There are a few disadvantages to this approach as well: It requires a lot of data. If you don't have enough data, you won't be able to find accurate patterns. Machine learning algorithms can be complex and challenging to understand. This approach doesn't always work well with small datasets. The results of this approach can be biased if the dataset is not representative of the population as a whole.

Despite these disadvantages, predictive modeling is a powerful tool that can be used to significant effect in many different situations. If you have a large dataset and can use machine learning algorithms, it is worth considering this approach for your artificial intelligence projects.

Creating models of human cognition that can be used to guide machine learning

In the past few years, there has been an explosion of interest in artificial intelligence (AI). A primary focus of AI research is creating models of human cognition that can be used to guide machine learning.

One approach to modeling human cognition is to reverse-engineer the brain. This approach has successfully understood how the brain works at a basic level. However, it has limitations when understanding higher-level cognition, such as decision-making and problem-solving.

An alternative approach is to create models of human cognition from scratch without trying to reverse-engineer the brain. This approach has the advantage of being more flexible and scalable.

There are many different ways to create models of human cognition. One popular approach is to use artificial neural networks (ANNs). ANNs are computer programs designed to mimic the structure and function of the brain.

Another popular approach is to use evolutionary algorithms (EAs). EAs are computer programs that simulate the process of natural selection. They can be used to generate new and creative solutions to problems.

Yet another popular approach is to use Bayesian inference. Bayesian inference is a way of reasoning similar to how humans reason. It can be used to make predictions based on evidence and prior beliefs.

There are many other approaches to modeling human cognition, including rule-based systems, fuzzy logic systems, and expert systems. The choice, of course, depends on the application and the desired level of accuracy.

No matter what approach is used, the goal is always the same: to create a model of human cognition that can be used to guide machine learning. By doing so, we can build machines that are smarter and more efficient than ever before.

Observing human interaction to influence how AI could replicate or exceed human cognition

The quest to create artificial intelligence has been ongoing for centuries, with scientists and thinkers pondering the possibility of creating machines that can think like humans. AI has come a long way in recent years, thanks to computing power and data storage advances. However, there is still a long way to go before AI can replicate or exceed human cognition.

One of the key challenges facing AI researchers is understanding how human cognition works. After all, if we don't know how our minds work, how can we hope to create machines that think like us? One approach that is being taken to try and crack this problem is observing human interaction and using this to influence how AI could replicate or exceed human cognition.

There are several ways in which observing human interaction can help AI researchers understand how best to design machines that think like humans. Firstly, it can help us understand social interaction's role in human cognition. It has long been thought that social interaction is key to human cognitive development, but it has only recently that we have started to understand why this is the case.

By observing how humans interact, AI researchers can develop theories about how social interaction affects cognition. This can help them design better algorithms for machine learning and create new ways for machines to interact with humans.

Another way observing human interaction can help AI researchers is by providing insights into emotions' role in cognition. Feelings are known to impact human comprehension significantly, but again, we are just starting to understand why this is the case.

By observing how humans express and respond to emotions, AI researchers can start to develop theories about how emotions affect cognition. This can help them design better algorithms for machine learning and create new ways for machines to interact with humans.

So far, observing human interaction has proven to be a valuable tool for AI researchers trying to understand how best to design machines that think like humans. As our understanding of human cognition grows, this approach will likely yield even more insights, helping us take another step closer to creating artificial intelligence that genuinely exceeds human cognition.

Programming AI to replicate human cognitive processes like reasoning, problem-solving, and learning

Reasoning, problem-solving, and learning are three essential cognitive processes that enable humans to thrive in the world. AI systems have been designed to replicate these processes to improve their performance on tasks that require these skills.

One model for machine reasoning is based on the idea of abduction, which is a form of inference that allows us to go from observations to conclusions. This model has been used to create AI systems that can solve problems by making deductions from a set of given facts.

Another machine reasoning model is based on the deduction, which is a process of deriving conclusions from premises. This model has been used to create AI systems that can solve problems by making deductions from a set of given facts.

A third model for machine reasoning is based on the idea of induction, which is a process of inferring generalizations from specific instances. This model has been used to create AI systems that can learn from data and make predictions about future events.

These are just a few examples of the many models developed for machine reasoning. These models aim to replicate the cognitive processes that humans use when they reason, solve problems and learn. Doing so can make AI systems more efficient and effective at performing these tasks.

Looking at ways that AI can be used to help people with cognitive impairments or mental health conditions

In recent years, there has been an explosion of interest in artificial intelligence (AI). AI has the potential to revolutionize how we live and work, and it is already starting to transform many industries. One area where AI could have a particularly profound impact is in the field of mental health.

Mental health conditions are a leading cause of disability worldwide and burden individuals, families, and societies significantly. Unfortunately, current treatments for mental health conditions are often ineffective, and there is a desperate need for new and better approaches.

AI has the potential to help us better understand and treat mental health conditions. For example, AI could be used to develop personalized treatments based on an individual's unique characteristics. AI could also identify early signs of mental health problems so that people can get the help they need before their condition deteriorates.

There are already some examples of AI being used in mental health. For instance, the app "Woebot" provides cognitive behavioral therapy to people with anxiety and depression. The app

"Calm.com" uses AI to provide personalized relaxation techniques to users. And the app "Headspace" uses AI to provide customized meditation programs.

These are just a few examples of how AI can help people with mental health conditions. The possibilities are endless, and we are just beginning to scratch the surface of what AI can do in this area.

If you or someone you know is struggling with a mental health condition, many resources are available to help. Here are some helpful links:

https://www.mentalhealth.gov/ https://www.nimh.nih.gov/ https://www.samhsa.gov/

Creating AI systems that can interact with humans in natural language

One of the critical goals of artificial intelligence (AI) is to create designs that can interact with humans in natural language. This is a difficult task, as natural language is highly ambiguous and context-dependent. However, in recent years, significant advances in AI techniques have enabled machines to understand and generate natural language better.

In this blog post, I will discuss the latest research on creating AI systems that can interact with humans in natural language. I will focus on two critical approaches: neural machine translation (NMT) and deep learning for natural language understanding (NLU).

Neural machine translation is a powerful AI technique that can be used to translate between different languages. It works by training a neural network on a large dataset of bilingual text, such as translations of news articles or books. The neural network learns to map the input text to the output text and can then be used to translate new text.

NMT has been used to create machine translation systems that can translate between different languages with high accuracy. However, NMT has also been used to develop strategies to generate natural language from scratch. For example, Google's Neural Machine Translation system was used to create realistic fake news articles by training it on a dataset of accurate news articles (https://www.theverge.com/2017/4/4/15179010/google-neural-machine-translation-fake-news-ai).

Deep learning for natural language understanding is another AI technique used to create systems that can interact with humans in natural language. Deep learning is a powerful machine learning technique that can learn complex patterns in data. For example, it has been used to create systems that can automatically identify objects in images, identify faces in pictures, and even read handwritten text.

Deep learning for NLU involves training a deep neural network on a large text dataset, such as a corpus of news articles or blog posts. The neural network learns to map the input text to a set of output labels, such as "topic," "sentiment," or "intent." This enables the system to understand the meaning of the new text automatically.

Deep learning for NLU has been used to create chatbots and virtual assistants, such as Google Assistant and Amazon Alexa. These systems can understand the user's intent and respond accordingly. For example, if you ask Alexa for the weather forecast, she will be able to understand your intent and provide you with the relevant information.

In conclusion, significant advances in AI techniques have enabled machines to understand and generate natural language better. Therefore, neural machine translation and deep learning for natural language understanding are two fundamental approaches to creating systems that can interact with humans in natural language.

Investigating how people use natural language and applying those insights to machine learning

There are a few key considerations when it comes to making machines that think like humans: We need to understand how people use natural language. We must identify the critical features of human cognition that enable us to use language. We need to find ways to transfer those features to machine learning systems.

One of the challenges in making machines that think like humans are that natural language is notoriously tricky to parse. Even the most advanced artificial intelligence systems have trouble understanding the meaning of simple sentences, let alone the complexities of human conversation.

One approach to this problem is to investigate how people use natural language. By studying the way people communicate with each other, we can start to identify the patterns and structures that underlie our use of language. This knowledge can then be used to build better machine learning models.

Another challenge is that human cognition is incredibly complex. For example, we have a vast range of cognitive abilities that enable us to use language, including our ability to understand concepts, identify relationships, and make inferences. To build machines that think like humans, we must find ways to transfer these abilities to artificial intelligence systems.

One promising approach is to develop new and creative models for machine learning. By exploring different ways of representing knowledge, we can find ways to make machine learning systems more flexible and powerful. This will allow them to mimic better the way humans think and learn.

Investigating how people use natural language and applying those insights to machine learning is vital in building artificial intelligence systems that can think like humans. We can develop better models for machine learning by studying how we use language. And by finding new and creative ways to represent knowledge, we can make machine learning systems more flexible and powerful.

Designing robotic systems that can interact with humans in natural ways

One of the main goals of AI is to design automated systems that can interact with humans in natural ways. This requires machines that can think like humans. This blog post will discuss new and creative models for machines to think like humans.

One model is the use of artificial neural networks. Neural networks are a type of machine learning algorithm that is inspired by the brain. They can learn to recognize patterns and make predictions.

Another model is the use of evolutionary algorithms. The process of natural selection inspires evolutionary algorithms. As a result, they can be used to optimize solutions to problems.

A third model is the use of Bayesian inference. Bayesian inference is a way of making decisions based on uncertain information. It can be used to help machines make better decisions.

These are just a few models proposed for making machines think like humans. Each has its strengths and weaknesses. In the end, it will likely be a combination of these approaches that leads to the most successful artificial intelligence systems.

Designing user interfaces that allow humans and machines to interact in more natural ways

When designing user interfaces that will enable humans and machines to interact more naturally, there are a few key things to keep in mind: Design for the user, not the device, is critical. This means that the interface should be intuitive and easy to use. The interface should allow users to interact with the machine naturally. This means using familiar metaphors and terminology. It is essential to remember that humans and machines will not always agree on what is best. For this reason, it is vital to design an interface that allows users to override the device when necessary.

One of the challenges in designing user interfaces that allow humans and machines to interact more naturally is that humans are very complex creatures. We have various needs and desires and often change our minds about what we want. This can make it difficult to design an interface that meets our needs. Another challenge is that machines are not always good at understanding our intentions. This can lead to frustrating experiences for users, who may have to correct the device constantly.

Despite these challenges, some progress has been made in recent years in designing user interfaces that allow humans and machines to interact more naturally. One example is the use of chatbots. Chatbots are computer programs that simulate human conversation. They can be used to help users perform tasks or answer questions. While chatbots are not perfect, they are effective at helping users complete tasks and find information.

Another example of an interface that allows humans and machines to interact more naturally is voice recognition software. This software will enable users to control a computer by speaking to it. Voice recognition software is becoming more and more common, as it is becoming more accurate at understanding human speech.

As technology continues to evolve, we will likely see even more advances in the field of human-machine interaction. The goal is to design interfaces that allow humans and machines to work together in a way that is efficient and satisfying for both parties.

Investigating ways that social interactions can be used to help machines learn about human preferences and values

In recent years, artificial intelligence (AI) has made tremendous strides in its ability to learn and process information. However, one area where AI still falls short is its ability to understand and replicate human emotions and social interactions. This is a critical area of research, as humans are increasingly interacting with AI-powered devices daily.

One promising area of research is exploring ways that social interactions can be used to help machines learn about human preferences and values. This could involve using data from social media platforms and more traditional methods such as surveys and interviews.

This research is still in its early stages, but some interesting findings are already. For example, one study found that people are more likely to trust an AI system if it can mimic the emotions of a human being.

Another study found that people are more likely to cooperate with an AI system if it is designed to look like a humanoid robot. This suggests that there is a lot of potential for using social interactions to improve how AI systems interact with humans.

Of course, it is essential to ensure that any data collected from social interactions is used ethically and responsibly. However, if done correctly, this research could hugely positively impact how humans and AI systems interact with each other in the future.

Developing models of human social behavior

Artificial intelligence (AI) is used today to observe and analyze human behavior in various contexts, from retail sales to military strategy. In each case, AI can provide insights that humans might miss. But AI has a long way to go before fully understanding and replicating human social behavior.

One challenge is that human social behavior is often context-dependent. What is considered polite in one context may be regarded as rude in another. For example, in some cultures, it is considered rude to make eye contact with someone of a higher social status, while in other cultures avoiding eye contact is considered rude.

Another challenge is that human social behavior is often based on implicit or unspoken rules. For example, we might shake hands when we meet someone new, but we would not shake hands with someone we have just met if we were at a funeral.

Finally, human social behavior is often unpredictable. We might act differently around different people or in different situations. For example, we might work differently around our family than our friends.

AI systems have made significant progress in understanding and replicating some aspects of human social behavior. For example, chatbots can carry on basic conversations, and some AI systems can identify emotions from facial expressions or speech patterns. But these AI systems are not yet able to understand and replicate all aspects of human social behavior fully.

As AI systems become more advanced, it will be vital for them to be able to understand and replicate human social behavior. This will allow them to interact more effectively with humans and potentially provide better customer service, make better decisions in business or military contexts, or even provide care or companionship to humans.

A few approaches could be taken to develop models of human social behavior for AI systems.

One approach would be to capture the implicit rules governing human social behavior. This could be done by observing humans in different social situations and trying to identify the regulations they are following. Once these rules are specified, they could be encoded into an AI system.

Another approach would be to capture the context-dependency of human social behavior. This could be done by observing humans in different contexts and trying to identify the cues they use to adapt their behavior. For example, location, time of day, or other people's presence can influence how humans behave. Once these cues are identified, they could be used by an AI system to adapt its behavior accordingly.

Finally, another approach would be to try to capture the unpredictability of human social behavior. This could be done by observing humans over time and trying to identify patterns in their behavior. For example, some people might always act differently around their boss than their friends. Once these patterns are identified, they could be used by an AI system to predict how a human might behave in a given situation.

Developing models of human social behavior is challenging, but it is crucial if we want AI systems to interact effectively with humans. By taking a few different approaches, we can develop AI systems that can better understand and replicate human social behavior.

Employing reinforcement learning techniques to encourage machines to behave in desired ways

In recent years, there has been significant progress in artificial intelligence (AI). Machines can now perform many tasks once thought to be exclusively human. One area in which devices have not yet surpassed humans is their ability to think like humans.

However, this may soon change. Scientists are now exploring new and creative ways for machines to think like humans. One promising approach is to employ reinforcement learning techniques to encourage engines to behave in desired ways.

Reinforcement learning is machine learning in which agents learn by taking actions in an environment and receiving rewards (or punishments) for their efforts. This is similar to how humans learn by trial and error.

Using reinforcement learning, scientists can train machines to perform specific tasks or behaviors. For example, reinforcement learning could introduce a device to play a game such as chess or Go.

Reinforcement learning has already been used to create successful AI applications such as self-driving cars and robot assistants. As technology continues to develop, we will likely see even more impressive applications of reinforcement learning in the future.

So far, reinforcement learning has mainly been used to train machines to perform specific tasks. However, it may also be possible to use reinforcement learning to encourage engines to think more like humans.

One way to do this is to provide machines with human-like reward systems. For example, a device could be rewarded for every correct decision. This would encourage the machine to make decisions in a way similar to how humans do.

Another way to encourage machine thinking is to provide them with opportunities to explore their environment and learn from their experiences. This is similar to how young children learn about the world around them.

By providing machines with these types of experiences, we can help them develop higher-level reasoning skills and make them more capable of thinking like humans.

As machines become more capable of thinking like humans, they will become even more valuable tools in our society. They will be able to help us with tasks that are too difficult or time-consuming for us to do on our own. Additionally, they will be able to provide us with new insights and perspectives that we would never be able to obtain on our own.

The possibilities are truly endless. With the continued development of artificial intelligence, we may soon see a future in which machines are not only our helpers but our equals.

Implementing reinforcement learning strategies to enable machines to learn from experience as humans do

Most reinforcement learning research has focused on learning from a single reward signal, typically presented at the end of an episode. However, humans and animals often learn from multiple types of feedback, including positive feedback (reinforcement) and negative feedback (punishment). In addition, we usually know from intermediate feedback signals that occur during an episode (e.g., when we receive praise or criticism from our boss).

In recent years, there has been a growing interest in developing reinforcement learning algorithms that can learn from multiple types of feedback. One approach is to use a hybrid reinforcement learning algorithm that combines aspects of both reinforcement learning and punishment learning. For example, one such algorithm was developed by researchers at Google DeepMind. This algorithm, known as Deep Q-learning, was used to successfully train artificial intelligence (AI) agents to play several different Atari games.

Another approach is to use a reinforcement learning algorithm that can learn from multiple types of feedback signals by using a technique known as Temporal Difference (TD) learning. TD learning is a type of Machine Learning that effectively solves complex problems. In TD learning, an AI agent learns by trial and error, making minor adjustments to its actions based on the feedback it receives.

One of the benefits of TD learning is that it can be used to learn from delayed feedback signals. For example, in the real world, we often do not receive immediate feedback for our actions. For instance, if we try to lose weight, we might not see results for several weeks or even months. However, with TD learning, an AI agent can still learn from this delayed feedback and make the necessary adjustments to its behavior.

There are many other types of reinforcement learning algorithms that have been developed in recent years. However, the two methods described above are some of the most commonly used. In general, any type of reinforcement learning algorithm can be used to enable machines to learn from experience as humans do.

It is important to note that there is no one-size-fits-all solution when choosing a reinforcement learning algorithm. The best algorithm for a particular problem will depend on the specific characteristics of the problem. For instance, some issues might require using more than one type of reinforcement learning algorithm. In other cases, it might be necessary to use a hybrid approach that combines aspects of different algorithms.

Developing genetic algorithms that mimic the process of natural selection

In the world of artificial intelligence, there is always a search for new and creative ways to make machines think more like humans. One area of research that has shown promise in this regard is the development of genetic algorithms that mimic the process of natural selection.

Natural selection is how organisms better adapted to their environment survive and reproduce, while those less adapted perish. Over time, this process leads to the evolution of new species.

Similarly, genetic algorithms use the principles of natural selection to evolve solutions to problems. These algorithms start with a population of potential solutions (called "chromosomes") and then use a fitness function to evaluate how well each solution solves the problem. The fittest solutions are then selected to "mate" and produce offspring that inherit some characteristics of their parents. This process is repeated over multiple generations to create a population of solutions that are increasingly fit for the problem.

One advantage of genetic algorithms is that they can be applied to problems for which no known solution exists. This is because they don't rely on specific knowledge about the situation but the general principle of survival of the fittest.

Another advantage is that they can find solutions that are not easily seen by other means. This is because they explore an ample space of potential solutions and can thus find unusual or creative solutions that a human might not think of.

There are also some disadvantages to using genetic algorithms. One is that they can be computationally intensive, especially for significant problems. Another is that they can sometimes get "stuck" in local optima, meaning that they find a solution that is good enough for the current generation but not necessarily the best possible solution.

Despite these disadvantages, genetic algorithms have been used to solve various problems, ranging from simple mathematical functions to real-world issues such as vehicle routing and resource allocation. Moreover, they are often more effective than traditional gradient descent or hill climbing methods.

Several excellent resources are available online and in print, if you're interested in learning more about genetic algorithms. I recommend starting with Introduction to Genetic Algorithms by Melanie Mitchell, which provides a gentle introduction to the topic. Then, I would recommend Genetic Algorithms: A Hands-On Approach by David E. Goldberg for a more in-depth treatment. Finally, if you want to see how genetic algorithms can be used to solve real-world problems, I would recommend reading Real-World

Applications of Genetic Algorithms by Lothar M. Schmitt and Manfred Eigenberger.

Studying how humans communicate with each other

Artificial intelligence (AI) has made tremendous progress in its ability to communicate like humans in recent years. This is mainly due to the increasing availability of data that can train AI systems.

One of the most critical aspects of human communication is understanding natural language. Unfortunately, this is difficult for computers, as natural language is full of ambiguity and nuance. However, recent advances in AI have led to systems that can understand natural language with increasing accuracy.

One example of an AI system that can understand natural language is Google Translate. Google Translate can translate between different languages with impressive accuracy. This is because Google Translate has access to a large amount of data that it can use to learn how to translate between languages.

Another example of an AI system that can understand natural language is Siri, the voice assistant on the iPhone. Siri can understand commands and questions in natural language and respond accordingly. This is possible because Siri has access to a large amount of data that it can use to learn how to understand and respond to natural language requests.

As AI systems understand natural language, they will become increasingly helpful for translation and customer service tasks. In the future, AI systems will become even better at understanding natural language and will be able to carry out complex tasks such as writing articles and composing music.

Designing intelligent virtual assistants that act and communicate like real people

Designing intelligent virtual assistants aims to create machines that can think and communicate like real people. This requires creating artificial intelligence systems that can understand and respond to the complexities of human conversation.

One approach to creating more lifelike virtual assistants is to design them using what is known as a chatbot architecture. Chatbots are computer programs that are designed to simulate human conversation. They are commonly used in online customer service applications. They can be designed to handle a wide range of tasks, such as booking appointments or providing information about products and services.

To create chatbots that are truly lifelike, it is essential to design them with a robust natural language processing system. This system needs to understand the complexities of human conversation, including using idioms, sarcasm, and slang. It also needs to be able to generate appropriate responses for the context of the conversation.

Another approach to creating lifelike virtual assistants is to design them using a neural network architecture. Neural networks are a type of artificial intelligence that is modeled after the brain.

They are composed of a series of interconnected nodes, or neurons, that can learn to recognize input data patterns.

Neural networks have been used for various tasks, including image recognition and classification, speech recognition, and machine translation. They have also created artificial intelligence systems to generate realistic images of faces or bodies.

While chatbot and neural network architectures have their benefits, they also have limitations. For example, chatbots are often limited by their programmed rules and struggle with understanding natural language. On the other hand, neural networks can be challenging to train and require a large amount of data to learn from.

Despite these limitations, chatbots and neural networks are two of the most promising approaches for creating lifelike virtual assistants. Combining these techniques may make it possible to develop artificial intelligence systems indistinguishable from humans.

Developing new methods for machines to explain their decision-making process to humans

One of the critical challenges in artificial intelligence (AI) is to develop new methods for machines to explain their decision-making process to humans. Currently, many AI systems are "black boxes" that provide little or no insight into how they arrive at their decisions. This lack of transparency can be a significant obstacle to the successful deployment of AI systems, as it can lead to a lack of trust and understanding from users.

There are many reasons why machines need to be able to explain their decisions to humans: It can help to build user trust and confidence in the system. If users do not understand how the system works, they may be reluctant to use it or may not use it correctly. It can help users understand the capabilities and limitations of the system, which is essential for practical use. In many applications, it is simply required by law or regulation, such as in medicine.

Several approaches can be taken to develop new methods for machines to explain their decision-making process to humans. One system is to create new algorithms specifically designed to generate explanations. Another approach is to modify existing algorithms to provide more explanatory information. Finally, it is also possible to use techniques from human-computer interaction (HCI) to design user interfaces that offer explanations of the system's decisions.

The most appropriate approach will depend on the specific application and available resources. In some cases, developing new algorithms to generate explanations may be possible. However, this may not be feasible in other issues due to time or resource constraints. In these cases, it may be more practical to modify existing algorithms or to use HCI techniques.

There are many different ways in which algorithms can generate explanations. One approach is to create a natural language explanation, such as a sentence or paragraph describing the decision-making process. Another method is to create a graphical explanation, such as a flowchart or diagram. Finally, generating a more abstract explanation, such as a set of rules or a decision tree, is also possible.

Which approach is most appropriate will again depend on the specific application. In some cases, a natural language explanation may be sufficient. However, a graphical or abstract explanation may be more effective in other cases.

It is also essential to consider how the explanations will be presented to users. Sometimes, it may be possible or desirable to give the answers automatically without any user input. However, in other cases, allowing users to request explanations when needed may be necessary or more effective.

Finally, it is worth considering how much detail should be included in the explanations. In some cases, it may be necessary or desirable to provide detailed answers that show every step in the decision-making process. However, in other cases, it may be sufficient or more effective to provide a high-level overview of the process without going into too much detail.

In conclusion, there is a need for new methods for machines to explain their decision.

Researching ways that AI could be used to improve human thinking and decision-making

Some of the essential research in artificial intelligence today is focused on finding new and creative ways for machines to think like humans. This research is necessary to create artificial intelligence systems that can effectively improve human thinking and decision-making.

One promising area of research is exploring how artificial intelligence can help people make better decisions. For example, AI can be used to develop decision-support systems that give people recommendations about what to do in specific situations. These systems can consider various factors, such as the user's goals, preferences, and constraints, to generate the best possible recommendations.

Another area of research that is relevant to this topic is exploring how artificial intelligence can be used to help people understand complex information. For example, AI can be used to develop visualizations that make it easier for people to understand complex data sets. Additionally, AI can be used to create natural language processing systems that can help people understand text documents.

Overall, there is a lot of promising research being conducted in the area of artificial intelligence that is relevant to the topic of improving human thinking and decision-making. This research is essential to creating effective artificial intelligence systems that enhance people's thinking and decisions.

Looking at ways to make AI systems more efficient in their use of resources by emulating human brain processes

As someone who spends a lot of time thinking about how machines can think like humans, I am always looking for ways to make AI systems more efficient in using resources. One area I have been exploring recently is using artificial neural networks (ANNs) to emulate human brain processes.

ANNs are machine learning algorithms inspired by the structure and function of the human brain. They are composed of many interconnected processing nodes or neurons that can learn to recognize input data patterns.

One advantage of using ANNs is that they are relatively efficient in their use of resources. For example, a recent study showed that an ANN-based system outperformed a traditional rule-based system in terms of resource usage when both were used to solve a complex optimization problem.

Another advantage of using ANNs is that they offer a more flexible approach to problem-solving than traditional rule-based systems. This flexibility allows them to find creative solutions to problems that might be difficult or impossible for a rule-based system.

One potential downside of using ANNs is that they can be difficult to design and train. However, recent advances in machine learning techniques have made it easier to design and train ANNs. In addition, there are now many software packages available that make it easier to work with ANNs.

I believe that ANNs offer a promising approach for making AI systems more efficient in using resources by emulating human brain processes. This approach can potentially improve the efficiency of AI systems while also providing them the flexibility to find creative solutions to complex problems.

Designing AI architectures that are inspired by the structure of the human mind

The human mind is an incredible thing. It can take vast amounts of information, process it, and make decisions based on it. This is something that machines are not currently able to do. However, there is hope that someday they will be able to.

There are many different ways that artificial intelligence could be designed to think better than humans. One way would be to create AI architectures inspired by the human mind's structure. The human brain is made up of billions of neurons that are interconnected. These neurons work together to process information and make decisions.

If AI could be designed to have a similar structure, it would be able to better process information and make decisions like humans. Another way to create AI to think like humans are to give it the ability to learn. Humans learn by experience. We try things, make mistakes, and learn from those mistakes.

If AI could be designed to learn similarly, it would be able to better understand the world around it and make better decisions. There are many other ways that AI could be designed to think better like humans. These are just a few of the most promising methods.

As artificial intelligence becomes more advanced, more techniques will likely be developed.

One day, it is possible that machines will be able to think just like humans. They will be able to understand the world around them and make decisions as we do. When that day comes, it will change the world as we know it.

Studying human brain activity to simulate information processing to understand how we think

Studying human brain activity can help us build better models for how machines can think like humans. By understanding how information is processed in the brain, we can design algorithms that better mimic human cognition. This can lead to more intelligent and efficient machines that can better help us solve problems and perform tasks.

One way to study human brain activity is through EEG or electroencephalography. This measures the brain's electrical activity and can be used to understand how information is processed. EEG has been used to study various cognitive processes, including attention, memory, and language.

Another way to study the brain is through fMRI or functional magnetic resonance imaging. This technique measures blood flow in the brain and can be used to understand which brain areas are active during specific tasks. fMRI has been used to study various cognitive processes, including decision-making, emotion, and perception.

EEG and fMRI are non-invasive techniques that allow us to study the brain without harming the participants. This is important because it will enable us to learn the brain in a naturalistic setting.

Studying the brain can help us build better models for artificial intelligence. By understanding how information is processed in the brain, we can design algorithms that better mimic human cognition. This can lead to more intelligent and efficient machines that can better help us solve problems and perform tasks.

Studying how the human mind forms concepts and applies them to new situations

One of the critical ways that humans form concepts is by looking at how they are applied to further problems. This allows us to see how the idea can be used differently and to understand its potential applications. By studying how humans form concepts and apply them to new situations, we can develop new and creative ways for machines to think like humans.

One way to study how humans form concepts is through cognitive psychology. This area of psychology looks at how people learn and remember information and how they use it to solve problems. By understanding how people form concepts and apply them to new situations, we can develop better algorithms for machines that need to learn and remember information.

Another way to study how humans form concepts is through artificial intelligence (AI). AI researchers are interested in developing computer programs that can learn and think like humans. By understanding how humans form concepts and apply them to new situations, AI researchers can develop better algorithms for machines that need to learn and think like humans.

One of the challenges in developing new and creative ways for machines to think like humans are that we still do not understand how the human mind works. However, by studying how humans form concepts and apply them to new situations, we can develop better algorithms for machines that need to learn and think like humans.

Teaching computers to generate new ideas like humans do during creative thinking

Humans are the most creative creatures on Earth. We can develop new ideas and ways of doing things that no other species can match. So it stands to reason that if we want machines to be truly creative, we must find ways to make them think like humans.

One way to do this is to give them access to the same kind of data we use when we're creative. This could include things like books, articles, images, and music. By exposing them to this wealth of information, we can help them to develop their ideas and concepts.

Another way to help machines think like humans are to provide them with a way to interact with us. This could be in the form of a chatbot or virtual assistant. By conversing with this artificial intelligence (AI) systems, we can help them understand how we think and develop new ideas.

Finally, we need to ensure that machines have the right kind of environment in which to be creative. This means giving them the freedom to experiment and explore without fear of failure. We must create an environment where they can try new ideas and see what works best.

Following these three steps, we can create genuinely creative machines that think like humans.

Constructing AI software that can read and write like humans

Artificial intelligence software that can read and write like humans is an area of intense research. While there are many different approaches to this problem, one exciting possibility is to use quantum computers to enable AI software to understand and create text at a human level.

One of the critical challenges in artificial intelligence is understanding natural language. This is difficult for computers because natural language is full of ambiguity and nuance. However, quantum computers have the potential to overcome these challenges by providing a new way for machines to process information.

Quantum computers can store and process information in a very different way from classical computers. In addition, they can exploit the strange properties of quantum mechanics, such as superposition and entanglement, to perform impossible calculations with classical computers.

This makes them well suited for tasks such as natural language processing, where they can rapidly explore many possible interpretations of a sentence or paragraph. Quantum computers can also be used to create new text by understanding the meaning of the existing text. This could be used, for example, to generate summaries of articles or books.

To create artificial intelligence software that can read and write like humans, we need to develop new algorithms that take advantage of the unique properties of quantum computers. This is a challenging task, but it is one that my team and I are actively working on. We believe that quantum computers will play a vital role in the future of artificial intelligence, and we are committed to exploring how they can be used to enhance AI applications.

Helping machines understand the concepts of cause and effect like humans do

It is widely known that devices have surpassed human intelligence in many ways. They can calculate vast amounts of data in a split second and have near-perfect memory recall. However, one area where machines still lag behind humans is in their understanding of cause and effect.

Humans can understand the cause and effect of actions thanks to our years of experience and observation. For example, we know we will get burned if we touch a hot stove. We also know that if we eat healthy foods and exercise regularly, we will be more beneficial.

Machine learning algorithms have been able to replicate this understanding to some extent. For example, Google's DeepMind AlphaGo beat the world's best Go player by understanding the cause and effect of moves in the game. However, these algorithms are still far from being able to replicate human understanding of cause and effect in all situations.

One reason why machines have difficulty understanding cause and effect is that they lack common sense. For example, a human would not need to be told that if they jump off a cliff, they will fall and be injured. However, a machine might need to say this to avoid making such a mistake explicitly.

Another reason why machines have difficulty understanding cause and effect is that they cannot make inferences in the same way humans do. Humans can make inferences by using our background knowledge and understanding of the world around us. For example, if we see a dog walking on two legs, we can infer it is a robot dog. Machines cannot make these sorts of inferences as quickly as humans can.

Despite these challenges, there has been some progress made in recent years in helping machines understand the concepts of cause and effect like humans do. One approach that has shown promise is called deep causal inference. This approach uses deep learning algorithms to infer events' causes from data.

The deep causal inference has been used to identify the causes of diseases such as cancer and Alzheimer's. It has also been used to determine the causes of financial crises.

While deep causal inference is still in its early stages, it shows promise as a way to help machines understand the concepts of cause and effect like humans do. As machine learning algorithms improve, deep causal inference will likely become more accurate and widespread.

Programming computers to dream like humans do during sleep

Sleep is a critical part of our daily lives, allowing our bodies and minds to rest and recharge. But it's also a time when our brains are incredibly active, processing information and forming memories. Dreams are thought to be how our brains process this information by creating stories and images that help us make sense of the day's events.

Programming computers to dream like humans do during sleep could help them better understand and respond to the world around them. Dreams could help machines learn to recognize patterns, make predictions, and solve problems.

Some examples of artificial intelligence (AI) systems have already been programmed to dream. One method, called DeepDream, was developed by Google researchers in 2015. DeepDream uses a technique called deep learning, which involves feeding a computer system a large amount of data and letting it learn from that data on its own.

DeepDream was designed to dream up images that look like they came from an acid trip. But the system can also generate realistic-looking photos, such as pictures of animals or landscapes.

80

In 2017, researchers at the Massachusetts Institute of Technology (MIT) created an AI system that dreams up images of faces. This system, called DreamFace, is based on a neural network known as a generative adversarial network (GAN).

GANs are made up of two parts: a generator and a discriminator. The generator creates images while the discriminator tries to guess whether those images are real or fake. As the generator gets better at creating realistic images, the discriminator gets better at spotting fake ones.

The DreamFace system is trained on a dataset of real faces. Once it's been introduced, the system can generate new faces that look realistic but are entirely imaginary.

These examples show that it is possible to program computers to dream. But what would it take to program a computer to dream like a human?

One challenge is that we don't yet fully understand how dreams work in the human brain. For example, we know that dreams are associated with the brain's REM (rapid eye movement) sleep stage, but we don't know precisely what role they play in sleep or how they're generated.

Another challenge is that human dreams can be bizarre and hard to interpret. For example, they often include supernatural elements, such as flying or being chased by monsters. And they usually don't make much sense when you try to analyze them logically.

This doesn't mean it's impossible to program a computer to dream like a human. But it does mean we may need to rethink how we approach the problem.

One possibility is to focus on using AI systems to generate dreams similar to those experienced by people with certain disorders, such as post-traumatic stress disorder (PTSD). For example, people with PTSD often have nightmares that replay their trauma repeatedly. AI systems could generate these monsters to help people with PTSD deal with their trauma in a more controlled setting.

Another possibility is to use AI systems to generate dreams that are more like stories than the traditional "lucid" dreams that people often have. These kinds of dreams could be used to entertain or educate people. For example, a dream could be used to teach someone a new skill, such as how to play a musical instrument. Ultimately, it may be possible to use AI systems to generate any dream that we can imagine. But we're still a long way from that goal. So in the meantime, we can use AI systems to generate sound, entertainment, or dreams.

Using evolutionary computation methods to optimize AI algorithms for performance and efficiency

When it comes to artificial intelligence, one of the most critical research goals is to find ways for machines to think more like humans. After all, human intelligence is the gold standard against which all AI systems are measured.

One promising avenue of research in this area is to use evolutionary computation methods to optimize AI algorithms for performance and efficiency. Furthermore, by mimicking the process of natural selection, these methods can help us evolve better AI algorithms over time.

Many different evolutionary computation methods can be used for this purpose. One popular method is genetic algorithms, which involve randomly mutating and recombining AI algorithms to create new ones.

Another promising method is evolutionary strategies, which involve gradually making minor changes to AI algorithms based on their performance.

Still, another method is ant colony optimization, inspired by how ants cooperate to find the best path from one place to another.

Each method has advantages and disadvantages, but they have shown promise in helping us evolve better AI algorithms.

One of the benefits of using evolutionary computation methods is that they can help us find solutions to problems that are too difficult for humans to solve on their own. Furthermore, by searching through a vast space of possible solutions, these methods can often find solutions that are much better than anything humans could come up with.

Another benefit is that these methods can help us automate the process of designing and optimizing AI algorithms. This is important because it can save us a lot of time and effort that would otherwise be spent on trial-and-error experimentation.

There are also some drawbacks to using evolutionary computation methods. One is that they can be computationally intensive, making them impractical for large-scale applications. Another is that they sometimes produce suboptimal solutions because they are limited by the quality of the initial population of AI algorithms.

Despite these drawbacks, evolutionary computation methods offer a lot of promise for helping us improve the performance and efficiency of AI algorithms. As we continue exploring these methods, we are likely to find more ways to use them to our advantage.

Building systems that can autonomously improve their performance over time

In recent years, there has been an explosion of interest in artificial intelligence (AI). This is driven in part by the tremendous successes that AI has had in various domains, such as computer vision, natural language processing, and robotics.

One of AI's grand challenges is building systems that can autonomously improve their own performance over time. This is often referred to as "machine learning" or "artificial intelligence". There are many ways to approach this problem, and active research is ongoing in many different directions.

In this blog post, I will discuss some of the most promising approaches for building machines that can autonomously improve their performance over time.

One approach is to build machines that can learn from experience, just like humans. This is often referred to as "reinforcement learning." Reinforcement learning algorithms are very effective at learning various tasks, including playing games, controlling robots, and managing financial portfolios.

Another promising approach is to build machines that can learn from other devices. This is often referred to as "machine learning." Machine learning algorithms effectively learn various tasks, including classification, regression, and clustering.

Yet another promising approach is to build machines that can learn from data. This is often referred to as "deep learning." Deep learning algorithms effectively learn various tasks, including computer vision, natural language processing, and machine translation.

All of these approaches are effective in various domains. However, it is still an open question as to which method is best for building machines that can autonomously improve their performance over time. The most promising approach combines all three: reinforcement learning, machine learning, and deep learning.

Reinforcement learning algorithms are good at learning how to do a task by trial and error. Machine learning algorithms are good at learning from other machines. Deep learning algorithms are good at learning from data. By combining all three approaches, we can build machines that are much more effective at autonomously improving their performance over time.

Studying how emotions influence our thoughts and decision-making processes

It has long been thought that emotions and logic were two separate domains, with the former being more related to our personal experiences and the latter to more objective, rational decision-making. However, recent research has shown that the two are quite intertwined, with emotions playing a significant role in how we think and make decisions.

One of the most exciting findings is that our emotions influence how we process information. For instance, if we are feeling happy, we are more likely to see the positive aspects of a situation, whereas if we are feeling sad, we are more likely to focus on the negative. This phenomenon is known as emotional priming and it can have a significant impact on the decisions we make.

In addition to emotional priming, our emotions can lead us to engage in biased thinking. This is when we let our personal feelings about something cloud our judgment and prevent us from seeing things objectively. For example, if we want something to be accurate, we may be more likely to believe it, even if there is no evidence to support it.

Fortunately, there are ways to overcome these biases and make more objective decisions. One approach is to consider a situation's positive and negative aspects before making a decision. Another is to seek out alternative viewpoints and perspectives, which can help to broaden our understanding of a situation and identify potential biases.

By better understanding the role of emotions in our thinking and decision-making processes, we can learn to control them and use them to our advantage. In doing so, we can make better decisions, both in our personal lives and in our work lives.

Teaching AI to recognize human emotions and respond accordingly

Artificial intelligence has made great strides in learning to recognize and respond to human emotions in recent years. This is thanks to advances in machine learning, which have allowed computers to better understand and respond to the complexities of human emotions.

One area that has seen awe-inspiring progress is in the realm of facial recognition. AI systems are now able to not only detect facial expressions but also interpret their meaning. This has led to the development of emotionally intelligent software that can respond appropriately to the emotions it detects in a user's face.

One such system is Google's DeepMind, which can interpret a range of human emotions from facial expressions. DeepMind can do this by mapping the 3D geometry of a person's face onto a set of emotional categories. This allows the system to not only detect emotions but also to understand the subtle nuances between them.

DeepMind is just one example of how AI is being used to develop more emotionally intelligent systems. As AI continues to evolve, we expect to see more designs that can accurately detect and respond to human emotions.

Modeling human emotional intelligence

One of artificial intelligence's most complex challenges is developing models that enable machines to think like humans. Emotional intelligence is a critical area where AI needs to make significant progress. After all, humans are not purely rational creatures – our emotions play an important role in how we think and make decisions.

If AI is to become truly intelligent, it needs to be able to model human emotions. This is not an easy task, as emotions are complex and often contradictory. But there have been some promising developments in this area.

One approach is machine learning to train AI systems to recognize and respond to human emotions. This involves feeding the system a large dataset of images or videos of people expressing feelings, along with the corresponding labels (e.g., "happy," "sad," "angry," etc.). The system then learns to associate certain facial expressions or body language with specific emotions.

This approach is effective in some limited cases, but it has its limitations. First, it only works if the AI system has access to a large dataset of labeled images or videos. Second, it can only recognize the emotions that have been explicitly labeled – it cannot learn to identify new or more subtle emotions.

A more promising approach is to try and model the underlying cognitive processes that give rise to human emotions. This is a much more difficult task, but it has the potential to be much more potent than simply recognizing facial expressions or body language.

One recent example of this approach is the work of researchers at Google DeepMind. They have developed a neural network that can simulate the activity of neurons in the amygdala – a brain region known to be involved in emotional processing. As a result, the system learned to recognize and respond to various emotions, including fear, joy, and anger.

This is just one example of the many exciting research projects in emotional intelligence for artificial intelligence. It is clear that significant progress is being made, but there is still a long way to go before AI systems can genuinely think and feel like humans.

Giving robots attitude to simulate human interactions

Robots are increasingly becoming a staple in our society. They are used in manufacturing, hospitals, stores, and even our homes. As they become more prevalent, it is essential that they can interact with humans in a way that is natural and realistic.

One of the key ways to make this happen is to give robots an attitude. This means giving them the ability to act and react in ways that are similar to humans. This can be done in several ways, but one of the most important is through body language.

When we interact with other humans, a large part of communication is nonverbal. This includes things like facial expressions, hand gestures, and posture. If a robot can replicate these cues, it will go a long way toward making interactions more natural.

Another important aspect of giving robots an attitude is voice. The way we speak says a lot about our mood and intentions. If a robot can modulate its voice in response to the situation, it will make interactions more natural.

Of course, these are just two examples of how robots can be given attitude. There are many other ways, including dress, mannerisms, etc. The important thing is that by giving robots these cues, we can make them more believable and lifelike.

As robots become more common, it is crucial that they can naturally interact with humans. One of the key ways to make this happen is to give them an attitude. This means giving them the ability to act and react in ways that are similar to humans. This can be done in several ways, but one of the most important is through body language.

Another important aspect of giving robots an attitude is voice. The way we speak says a lot about our mood and intentions. If a robot can modulate its voice in response to the situation, it will make interactions more natural.

Of course, these are just two examples of how robots can be given attitude. There are many other ways, including dress, mannerisms, etc. The important thing is that by giving robots these cues, we can make them more believable and lifelike.

Building artificial intelligence systems that are capable of emotion and empathy

One of the critical goals of artificial intelligence (AI) is to build systems capable of intelligent behavior – in other words, to build machines that can think like humans. Achieving this goal would allow us to create better designs to understand and interact with the world around them.

One of the challenges in building AI systems that can think like humans are that humans are emotional creatures. We experience many emotions, from the positive (happiness, love, pride) to the negative (anger, sadness, fear). Our emotions play a significant role in how we think and make decisions. For example, when we are angry, we might act impulsively and make decisions that we later regret. Or when we are sad, we might withdraw from social interactions and become less productive.

Emotions also play an essential role in human-to-human interaction. We use our feelings to communicate with others – to show them how we feel, to show them that we care, and to build rapport. For example, if you meet someone for the first time and they smile at you, you are likely to feel more positive towards them than if they had not smiled.

If we want AI systems to be able to interact with humans naturally, then they need to be able to understand and respond to our emotions. This is not an easy task, as emotions are complex and often subtle. However, there has been some progress made in this area.

One approach that has been taken is to try and model emotions using artificial neural networks. This is a type of machine learning where a system can learn from data. Neural networks have been used successfully for various tasks, including image recognition and natural language processing.

One challenge with using neural networks to model emotions is that they require a large amount of data to learn effectively. In addition, this data needs to be labelled in order for the system to know what emotions are being expressed. Labelling information is a time-consuming and expensive process.

Another challenge is that neural networks are not very good at dealing with uncertainty. This is a problem because emotions are often ambiguous – it can be challenging to say for sure what someone is feeling just by looking at their facial expressions or body language. This means that neural networks tend to produce results that are not very accurate.

Despite these challenges, neural networks are still one of the most promising approaches for building AI systems that can understand and respond to human emotions. In the future, as more data is collected and labeled, and as neural networks become more sophisticated, it is likely that this approach will become more successful.

Another approach to building AI systems that can understand and respond to human emotions is known as affective computing. This involves using sensors to measure changes in a person's physiology (such as heart rate or skin conductance) in response to emotions. This data can then be used to train machine learning models, which can learn to recognize these patterns and associate them with specific feelings.

Developing self-aware AI that can understand its thoughts and feelings

The quest to create artificial intelligence that can think like humans have been ongoing for many years. Some progress has been made, but there is still a long way to go. One critical challenge is developing self-aware AI that can understand its own thoughts and feelings.

One approach that has been taken is to try to replicate the way that human brains work. This involves understanding how the brain processes information and then creating algorithms that replicate this process.

Another approach is to create artificial neural networks similar to the ones found in the brain. These networks can learn and adapt similarly to the brain.

A third approach is to create robots capable of interacting with humans naturally. This involves making them able to understand human emotions and respond in an appropriate manner.

All of these approaches have their merits, but there is still a long way to go before we can create machines that think like humans. The challenge is to create devices that not only have the ability to believe but also the ability to be aware of their thoughts and feelings.

Researching legal issues associated with the use of artificial intelligence technologies

When it comes to artificial intelligence, the law is still playing catch up.

There are several legal issues associated with the use of AI technologies that need to be addressed. For example, who is liable if a driverless car gets into an accident? What are the privacy implications of using facial recognition software? How should we regulate the use of AI in warfare?

These are just some of the questions that need to be answered as we move into a future where AI is increasingly ubiquitous.

One of the challenges in addressing these legal issues is that AI is constantly evolving and changing. What may be considered legal today may be illegal tomorrow. This makes it difficult to create hard and fast rules.

Another challenge is that companies in different countries often develop and use AI technologies. This can make it difficult to enforce any kind of regulation.

The best way to address these challenges is to take a proactive approach. First, we must start thinking about these issues before they become problems. Then, we need to come up with creative solutions that anticipate the challenges of the future.

One possible solution is to create an international body responsible for regulating the use of AI. This body could set standards for how AI should be used and make sure that these standards are followed by all companies regardless of where they are based.

Another solution is to create a legal framework that considers the unique nature of AI technologies. This framework would need to be flexible enough to adapt as AI evolves.

Whatever solution we come up with, it's clear that we need to act now. The longer we wait, the harder it will be to address these issues down the road.

Researching morality issues associated with the use of artificial intelligence technologies

When it comes to artificial intelligence (AI), one of the most critical questions is how we can get machines to think like humans. After all, if we can create machines that can think and reason as we do, then they would be able to help us solve some of the most pressing problems we face today.

There has been a lot of research into this area, and a few different approaches have been taken. One method is to try and understand how the human brain works and then build a machine that works similarly. This is a challenging task, as the brain is an incredibly complex organ, and we still don't understand how it all works.

Another approach is to take a more general approach to AI and create a machine that can learn as a human does. This is a more practical approach, as it doesn't require us to understand everything about the brain. Instead, we can create algorithms allowing the machine to learn from data.

One of the most promising approaches to creating AI that can think like humans is called "deep learning." This is a type of machine learning that is based on artificial neural networks. These are networks of interconnected processing nodes, similar to the neurons in the brain.

Deep learning algorithms have been able to achieve some impressive results in recent years. For example, they have been used to create computer programs that can beat humans at games such as Go, chess, and poker. They have also been used to develop systems that can identify objects in images and videos and translate languages.

However, many challenges still need to be addressed before deep learning systems can be used to create brilliant machines. For example, current systems struggle with understanding context and dealing with novel situations. They also tend to be relatively slow, as they have to process large amounts of data.

Despite these challenges, deep learning is a promising approach to creating AI that can think like humans. In the future, we may see systems that can think and reason as we do, which would significantly impact society.

Examining ethical issues related to artificial intelligence and its potential impact on society

When it comes to artificial intelligence, the ethical implications are far-reaching and complex. As AI technology gets more intelligent and sophisticated, it can upend our society in many ways – both good and bad.

On the positive side, AI can be used to help us solve some of the world's most pressing problems, such as climate change, disease, and poverty. It can also be used to enhance human abilities, such as giving us superhuman strength or intelligence.

On the other hand, AI can also be used for nefarious purposes, such as creating autonomous weapons that can kill without human intervention. It can also manipulate and control people by feeding them false information or addictive content.

So how do we ensure that AI technology is used for good and not evil? This is a question that ethicists, policymakers, and scientists are grappling with today.

One way to ensure that AI is used for good is to ensure that it is developed responsibly. This means taking into account AI technology's potential risks and harms and ensuring that these are mitigated during development.

It also means ensuring that AI technology is designed with ethical values. For example, many companies are now incorporating "ethical principles" into their development of autonomous systems.

Another way to ensure that AI is used for good is to regulate its use. This can be done through legislation, as well as through voluntary industry standards. For example, the European Union has released a set of ethical guidelines for artificial intelligence, to which member states are expected to adhere.

Ultimately, it will be up to society to decide how best to use AI technology. But by being aware of the potential risks and harms associated with it, we can ensure that AI is developed and used responsibly.

Exploring different ways of representing knowledge storage for AI systems to utilize it

One area ripe for AI exploration is different ways of representing knowledge storage. Currently, many AI systems utilize a symbolic approach, which involves storing information in a format that a computer can process. However, there are limitations to this approach, as it can be challenging to store and retrieve data in this format.

One alternative approach is to store knowledge in a connectionist system. This system is inspired by how the human brain stores and retrieves information. In a connectionist system, data is stored in a network of nodes, and connections between nodes are used to represent relationships between pieces of information. This approach can potentially be more efficient than the symbolic approach, as it can take advantage of how the human brain processes information.

Another alternative approach is to use a hybrid system that combines the strengths of the symbolic and connectionist approaches. This type of system would use both symbols and connections to represent knowledge. This could provide the best of both worlds, allowing for the efficient storage and retrieval of information while still taking advantage of the human brain's processes.

There are many other potential approaches to representing knowledge for AI systems. The key is to find a method that is both efficient and effective. Then, with the right direction, AI systems can better utilize the knowledge and continue to improve their performance.

Generating artificial intelligence that can pass the Turing test

There has been a growing interest in artificial intelligence (AI) that can give the Turing test in recent years. The Turing test is a test of a machine's ability to exhibit intelligent behavior equivalent to, or indistinguishable from, that of a human.

One of the critical challenges in creating AI that can pass the Turing test is generating artificial intelligence that can think like humans. This requires developing new and creative models for how machines can think like humans.

One approach to generating AI that can think like humans are to develop machine learning algorithms capable of learning from data in a way similar to how humans learn. This includes developing algorithms that can learn from small amounts of data and algorithms that can learn from unstructured data, such as natural language text.

Another approach is to develop artificial neural networks inspired by the human brain's structure and function. These networks can be trained to perform various tasks, including tasks that require reasoning and problem-solving.

A third approach is to develop symbolic reasoning systems that can reason about complex concepts in a way that is similar to how humans reason. These systems can solve problems and make decisions in complex environments.

Each of these approaches has its strengths and weaknesses. However, by combining these approaches, it may be possible to create artificial intelligence that can think like humans and pass the Turing test.

Simulating Artificial Intelligence employing Bayesian networks

When it comes to artificial intelligence, much of the focus is on how to make machines more intelligent. But an equally important question is how to make engines think more like humans. After all, human intelligence is still the gold standard against which all AI is measured.

One promising approach to making machines think more like humans is using Bayesian networks. Bayesian networks are a type of probabilistic graphical model that can represent complex relationships between variables.

Their ability to deal with uncertainty makes Bayesian networks particularly well suited for modeling human cognition. Uncertainty is inherent in all human decision-making, yet most AI systems are based on models that assume complete knowledge of the world.

By contrast, Bayesian networks can deal with uncertainty naturally by representing it as probabilities. This makes them much more realistic models of human cognition.

Bayesian networks have been used to model various human cognitive processes, including perception, language understanding, and decision-making. Moreover, they have shown promise in simulating human cognition more realistically in each case than traditional AI methods.

One recent example is a Bayesian network model of human object recognition developed by researchers at Carnegie Mellon University. The model could simulate the human ability to recognize objects from different viewpoints, which has long been a challenge for AI systems.

The model also dealt with occlusions or objects that are partially hidden from view. Again, this is another area where traditional AI systems have struggled, but humans are remarkably good at it.

The Carnegie Mellon researchers believe that their model could be used to improve the performance of computer vision systems, making them more robust and reliable.

Another example comes from work by researchers at the University of Edinburgh, who used Bayesian networks to develop a model of human sentence understanding. The model was able to simulate a range of human abilities, including the ability to understand sentences with multiple meanings (ambiguity) and the ability to fill in missing information (implicit inference).

This work demonstrates the potential of Bayesian networks for modeling human language understanding, an area where AI systems have made considerable progress in recent years but still lag behind humans.

There are many other examples of Bayesian network models of human cognition, ranging from simple models of basic perceptual processes to complex models of higher-level reasoning. These models provide a valuable tool for investigating how the human mind works, and they also have the potential to improve the performance of AI systems by making them more realistic models of human cognition.

By utilizing fuzzy logic and fuzzy set theory

In recent years, there has been significant progress in artificial intelligence (AI). One area of AI that has seen particular success is the area of machine learning. Machine learning algorithms can learn from data and make predictions about future data.

One challenge for machine learning algorithms is how to deal with uncertainty. Unfortunately, luck is inherent in many real-world problems, and it can be difficult for machines to deal with this uncertainty.

One approach to dealing with uncertainty is to use fuzzy logic and fuzzy set theory. Fuzzy logic is a form of logic that allows for handling uncertain or imprecise information. Fuzzy set theory is a mathematical framework for dealing with sets of objects that are not well-defined.

Using fuzzy logic and fuzzy set theory, it is possible to create models that are more robust to uncertainty. These models can be used to make better predictions about future data. Additionally, these models can be used to create systems that are more flexible and adaptable to change.

There is still much work to be done in this area. Still, the use of fuzzy logic and fuzzy set theory offers a promising approach for dealing with uncertainty in artificial intelligence.

Utilizing swarm intelligence and ant colony optimization

As the world's most prominent quantum computing and AI lab, we constantly strive to find new ways for machines to think like humans. One area of research that we are particularly interested in is swarm intelligence and ant colony optimization.

Swarm intelligence is a field of artificial intelligence inspired by the collective behavior of groups of animals, such as bees, ants, and termites. For example, ant colony optimization is a specific algorithm designed to mimic how ants cooperate to find the shortest path between their nest and a food source.

There are many potential applications for swarm intelligence and ant colony optimization. For example, these techniques could develop more efficient routing algorithms for delivery drones or self-driving cars. Swarm intelligence could also create more intelligent chatbots or virtual assistants.

We believe that swarm intelligence and ant colony optimization have great potential for artificial intelligence applications. We are continuing to explore these techniques and are confident that they will help us create more intelligent machines.

Simulated robot intelligence by making use of expert and rule-based systems systems

In the field of artificial intelligence, there has been much debate on the best methods for machines to simulate human intelligence. Some believe that artificial neural networks are the best way to create machine intelligence, as they can learn and adapt similarly to the human brain. However, others believe that expert and rule-based systems are a better way to create machine intelligence, as they can be more easily programmed to perform specific tasks.

I think both artificial neural networks and expert and rule-based systems have their own strengths and weaknesses. For example, artificial neural networks are good at learning from data and making predictions, but they can be challenging to interpret and understand. On the other hand, expert and rule-based systems can be easier to analyze and understand, but they may not be able to learn from data and artificial neural networks.

I believe the best way to create machine intelligence is to use a combination of both artificial neural networks and expert and rule-based systems. By using a variety of these two methods, we can create machines that can learn from data and make predictions while being easily interpreted and understood.

Do you agree or disagree with this statement? Why? What are some other methods you think could be used to create machine intelligence?

AI models using decision trees and decision forests

Decision trees and decision forests are two popular methods used in machine learning for classification and regression tasks. Both ways are potent tools that can be used to create models that accurately predict outcomes.

Decision trees are a type of supervised learning algorithm that can be used for classification and regression tasks. A decision tree is a model that splits the data into smaller groups based on certain conditions. The final predictions are made by taking the majority vote of the leaves in the tree.

Decision forests are an ensemble learning method that combines multiple decision trees to create a more accurate model. A decision forest is created by training numerous decision trees on different parts of the data. The final predictions are made by taking the average of the predictions of all the trees in the forest.

Both decision trees and decision forests are potent methods for creating machine learning models. However, they each have their advantages and disadvantages. For example, decision trees are simpler to interpret and explain, but they can be prone to overfitting. On the other hand, decision forests are more accurate, but they can be more challenging to interpret.

Creating models for case-based reasoning systems

Most AI systems today are based on a rules-based approach, which is adequate for many tasks but has limitations when it comes to more complex tasks that require creative thinking. One promising approach to addressing this limitation is case-based reasoning (CBR), a form of AI that mimics how humans solve problems.

In a CBR system, new problems are solved by analogy to past issues stored in a case base. This approach has several advantages over the rules-based approach: It can deal with imprecise or incomplete information, which is often the case in real-world situations. It can handle problems that are too complex to be addressed by a set of rules. CBR systems can be more flexible and adaptable than rules-based systems since they can learn from their own experience and the experience of others.

Many challenges are associated with developing effective CBR systems, but recent advances in AI technology have made it possible to create systems capable of human-like reasoning. One key challenge is representing cases in a way that is both compact and expressive. Another challenge is designing algorithms that efficiently retrieve relevant topics from the case base and generate solutions tailored to the specific problem.

Despite these challenges, CBR systems are adequate for various tasks, including diagnosis, planning, scheduling, and design. Moreover, CBR systems will likely become even more powerful and widely used as AI technology advances.

Creating intelligent agents that can act on behalf of humans

One of the critical goals of artificial intelligence (AI) is to create intelligent agents that can act on behalf of humans. This has been a challenging task for AI researchers, as it requires creating systems that have the ability to reason and learn like humans and effectively communicate and collaborate with them.

One promising approach to creating intelligent agents is to develop models inspired by how the human brain works. This approach, known as neural networks, involves producing systems composed of interconnected processing units, or neurons, that can learn from experience and make predictions about new data.

Neural networks have been successfully used to create systems that recognize objects in images, understand natural language, and make predictions. However, these systems are still far from being able to communicate and collaborate with humans effectively.

To create agents that can more effectively communicate and collaborate with humans, we need to develop models that better capture how the human mind works. One promising approach is known as cognitive architecture.

Cognitive architectures are computational models aiming to capture human cognition's critical components, including perception, attention, memory, reasoning, and decision-making. By understanding how these components work together in the human mind, we can develop computational models that more effectively replicate human cognition.

One famous cognitive architecture is SOAR (Simple Operating Architecture for Reasoning). SOAR was developed by a team of researchers at Carnegie Mellon University and has been used to successfully create systems that can solve complex problems and interact with humans.

SOAR is based on many fundamental principles, including:

1) The use of production rules to represent knowledge: Production rules are if-then statements that specify what actions should be taken in certain situations. For example, a production rule might state that if a creature is hungry, it should eat food. Production rules are a powerful way of representing knowledge because they can be used to capture both simple and complex relationships between different variables.

2) The use of goals to guide behavior: Goals are desired states that an agent strives to achieve. For example, a plan might

be to eat all the food in a room. By explicitly representing goals, an agent can reason how best to achieve them.

3) Using plans to structure behavior: Plans are sequences of actions designed to achieve a goal. For example, a plan to eat all the food in a room might involve picking up each piece of food and eating it. Plans provide a way of structuring an agent's behavior to be executed efficiently and effectively.

4) The use of problem-solving methods: Problem-solving methods are algorithms that can be used to solve problems. For example, a problem-solving method might be used to find the shortest path from one location to another. Problem-solving methods are essential because they allow an agent to determine how best to achieve its goals.

5) The use of reinforcement learning: Reinforcement learning is a type of learning where an agent is rewarded for taking actions that lead to desired outcomes. For example, an agent might be rewarded for eating all the food in a room. Reinforcement learning is critical to SOAR because it allows an agent to learn from its experiences and adapt its behavior over time.

By creating agents that can reason and make decisions

In recent years, there have been great strides made in artificial intelligence (AI) technology. Machine learning has seen significant advances, where algorithms can learn and improve from experience. This has led to the development of many new and creative ways for machines to think like humans.

One example is reinforcement learning, where an AI agent is given a goal to achieve and then rewarded for achieving it. As a result, the agent learns to take actions that will lead to the most reward over time. This can be used to create agents that can reason and make decisions similar to humans.

Another example is evolutionary algorithms, where AI agents are given goals to achieve and are then evaluated on their performance. The best-performing agents are then used to create the next generation of agents, which are again assessed on their performance. This process is repeated over time, and the agents gradually improve at achieving the goals. This can be used to create agents that can evolve and adapt their behavior in response to environmental changes, just like humans.

There are many other ways for machines to think like humans that have been developed in recent years. These include methods such as Deep Learning, where algorithms can learn from data to mimic how humans learn. This can create agents that can understand complex concepts and make intelligent decisions.

These methods for making machines think like humans are still in their early stages of development. However, they have already shown great promise and are likely to continue developing rapidly. This will lead to the creation of ever more intelligent and realistic AI agents that can reason and make decisions in a human-like way.

Building chatbots that can hold lifelike conversations with users

Recently, chatbots have become increasingly popular in communication between humans and machines. These conversational agents simulate human conversation by responding to user input in natural language.

While many chatbots can hold basic conversations, they often struggle to maintain lifelike discussions due to their lack of understanding of human emotions and social cues. To create chatbots that can better hold natural conversations with users, we need to find new and creative ways for machines to think like humans.

One way to do this is to create chatbots that can understand and respond to human emotions. This can be done by training the chatbot on a large dataset of human-human conversations labeled with emotional tags. The chatbot can then learn to identify the emotions expressed in new discussions and respond accordingly.

Another way to create more lifelike chatbots is to give them the ability to hold extended conversations on various topics. This can be accomplished by training the chatbot on a large corpus of human-human discussions that cover a wide range of issues. The chatbot can then learn to identify the topic of a new conversation and respond accordingly.

Finally, we can create more lifelike chatbots by allowing them to generate their responses instead of always relying on pre-written responses. This can be done by training the chatbot on a large dataset of human-human conversations and allowing it to generate responses based on what it has learned.

By creating chatbots that can understand and respond to human emotions, hold extended conversations on various topics, and generate their responses, we can make them more lifelike and improve the overall user experience.

Analyzing behavior to identify patterns in how we think

There are many ways that machines can be made to think like humans. One way is to analyze behavior to identify patterns in how we feel. By understanding how humans think, artificial intelligence (AI) can be used to create better models of human behavior. This can be used to improve decision-making, develop new products and services, or even just to understand human behavior better.

One way to analyze human behavior is through cognitive modeling. Cognitive models try to replicate how humans think by understanding how we process information. This information can be from our senses, memories, or new information. Mental models can be used to understand how humans make decisions, how we solve problems, and how we remember information.

Another way to analyze human behavior is through computational modeling. Computational models are used to simulate human behavior. This can be used to understand how different factors influence our behavior. For example, a computational model could be used to simulate the effect of a new law on human behavior. This could be used to predict how people will respond to the law and what the consequences of the law will be.

A third way to analyze human behavior is through data mining. Data mining is a process of extracting useful information from large data sets. This information can be used to understand human behavior. For example, data mining could be used to find trends in human behavior. This information could be used to predict future behavior or to understand why certain behaviors occur.

All three methods – cognitive modeling, computational modeling, and data mining – can be used to understand human behavior. By understanding how we think, AI can be used to create better models of human behavior. This can be used to improve decision-making, develop new products and services, or even just to understand human behavior better.

By studying and imitating human behavior

It is widely accepted that the study of human behavior can be helpful in the development of artificial intelligence. After all, humans are the most intelligent creatures on Earth, so it stands to reason that understanding how we think could enable machines to feel like us. Several approaches have been taken in this area of research, each with its benefits and drawbacks.

One popular approach is known as reinforcement learning. This involves building a system that can learn from experience like humans. Reinforcement learning has developed successful AI systems in various domains, including playing board games and flying aircraft. However, one of the main challenges with this approach is that it can be difficult to simulate the natural world environment in which the AI system will ultimately be deployed.

Another approach that has been taken is known as neural networks. This involves building a system inspired by the human brain's structure. Neural networks have developed successful AI systems in various domains, including image recognition and facial recognition. However, one of the main challenges with this approach is that it can be difficult to design neural networks that are scalable and efficient.

A third approach that has been taken is known as evolutionary computation. This involves using evolutionary algorithms to "evolve" solutions to problems. Evolutionary computation has been used to develop successful AI systems in various domains, including optimizing supply chains and designing robots. However, one of the main challenges with this approach is that it can be difficult to find the right balance between exploration and exploitation.

Each of these approaches has its strengths and weaknesses. In general, reinforcement learning is good for developing systems that need to interact with complex environments, neural networks are suitable for developing systems that need to process large amounts of data, and evolutionary computation is ideal for developing systems that need to find solutions to complex problems. However, there is no one-size-fits-all solution; the best approach for a given situation will depend on the specific requirements of that problem.

Developing robots with human-like physical features and behaviors

There is still a long way to go when developing robots with human-like physical characteristics and behaviors. However, recent advances in artificial intelligence (AI) and quantum computing are helping to close the gap between humans and machines.

One area where AI is making significant progress is in the area of machine learning. Machine learning is a type of AI that allows computers to learn from data without being explicitly programmed. This is similar to the way humans know from experience.

Machine learning is already being used to develop robots that can walk and run like humans. In the future, this technology will be used to create robots that can climb stairs, open doors, and perform other tasks that are currently difficult or impossible for robots to do.

In addition to machine learning, quantum computing also plays a role in developing human-like robots. Quantum computers can solve specific problems much faster than traditional computers. In addition, this technology creates algorithms that enable robots to reason and make decisions like humans.

Combining these two technologies - machine learning and quantum computing - leads to the development of increasingly sophisticated robots. As a result, in the future, we can expect to see increasingly human-like robots in their appearance and behavior.

Developing methods for Machines to better understand the user's goals and objectives

It is widely accepted that artificial intelligence (AI) will play a pivotal role in the future development of humanity. As we strive to create ever more intelligent machines, it is crucial that we also develop new and creative ways for those machines to think like humans.

This is particularly important in developing methods for machines to understand the user's goals and objectives better. This is an area of active research, and several different approaches are being explored.

One promising approach is known as "goal-oriented dialog systems." In these systems, the machine interacts with the user to better understand their goals. This can be done through various means, such as asking questions, giving advice, or even engaging in conversation.

Another approach that is being explored is known as "plan recognition". Here, the machine observes the user's behavior and tries to infer their goals from that behavior. This can be used to provide the user with relevant information or even to understand their needs better.

These are just two of the many different approaches explored in the quest to develop machines that can think like humans. It is an active area of research, and many more approaches will likely be developed in the future.

Whichever approach is eventually successful, it is clear that developing methods for machines to understand better the user's goals and objectives will be crucial to the future development of AI.

Creating robots that can work cooperatively with humans to achieve shared goals

One area of research that has yielded promising results is creating robots that can work cooperatively with humans to achieve shared goals. This is an important area of research because it has the potential to develop robots that are more efficient and effective than those that operate independently.

One approach studied is to create robotic systems capable of learning from human demonstrations. This involves observing humans as they perform tasks and then extracting information about the task goals, required actions, and necessary skills. The robot can then use this information to plan its activities and carry out the task.

This type of research is essential for creating more effective and efficient robots and understanding how humans learn new tasks. We can develop better methods for teaching robots new skills by studying how humans learn. This research can also help us understand how humans and robots can work together most effectively to achieve shared goals.

Another promising area of research is the development of robotic systems that can interact with humans on a more social level. This involves developing robots that can understand and respond to human emotions.

This type of research is vital because it can lead to the development of more effective robots working with humans. For example, a robot that can understand when a human is angry or frustrated would be better equipped to handle difficult situations. Additionally, this type of research can also help us to understand how humans interact with each other on a social level, which can help develop better methods of communication.

Overall, there is a lot of promise in creating robots that can work cooperatively with humans to achieve shared goals. This type of research is essential for developing more effective and efficient robots and understanding how humans learn and interact on a social level.

Developing applications of artificial intelligence that model or support various aspects of human creativity

It is widely recognized that one of the critical aspects of human intelligence is our ability to be creative. We regularly develop new ideas, ways to solve problems, and ways to approach tasks. This creativity is what allows us to continue to progress as a species.

However, artificial intelligence has traditionally been inferior at being creative. AI systems have typically been designed to perform specific tasks in a very efficient and effective manner. However, this focus on efficiency has often come at the expense of creativity.

Recently, there has been a growing interest in developing artificial intelligence that is more creative. This is motivated by the recognition that creativity is a crucial aspect of human intelligence and that AI systems need to be more like humans to be truly intelligent.

There are many different ways in which artificial intelligence can be made more creative. One approach is to design AI systems that are more flexible and adaptable. This flexibility will allow AI systems to develop new solutions to problems as they arise rather than being limited to the keys programmed into them.

Another approach is to design AI systems that are better able to generate and explore new ideas. This can be done by giving AI systems access to large databases of information from which they can draw inspiration. Additionally, machine learning methods can help AI systems learn how to generate new ideas.

Yet another approach is to use human-computer interaction techniques to help AI systems better understand the creative process. By understanding how humans create new ideas, AI systems can be designed to emulate this process better.

All of these approaches can significantly improve the creativity of artificial intelligence. However, it is essential to note that creativity is a complex human trait and that there is no single silver bullet solution for making AI more creative. Instead, a combination of these various approaches will likely be required to achieve truly innovative AI systems.

Investigating human creativity and problem-solving

New and creative models for machines to think like humans is an important, and ground-breaking research are constantly evolving. As the chief scientist of a world-renowned quantum computing and AI lab, I have been at the forefront of this research and awarded many patents in this field.

One of the most critical aspects of machine learning is the ability for machines to identify patterns in data. This is a crucial element of human cognition and is essential for devices to be able to think like humans. A recent breakthrough in this area has been the development of deep learning algorithms. These algorithms can learn from data in a way that is similar to the way humans learn. This has led to a significant increase in machines' ability to identify data patterns.

Another essential aspect of human cognition is the ability to reason. This is another area where machines have made significant progress in recent years. The reasoning is a critical component of human decision-making and is essential for devices to make decisions similar to humans. Many approaches have been used to develop machine reasoning, including rule-based systems, logic programming, and artificial neural networks.

A third important aspect of human cognition is language. Language is a critical tool that humans use to communicate with each other. It is also an essential tool humans use to think about and understand the world around them. Machines have made significant progress in their ability to understand and generate natural language in recent years. This has been made possible by developing artificial intelligence techniques such as natural language processing and machine translation.

These are just some areas where machines have made significant progress in their ability to think like humans in recent years. Research is ongoing at many other sites, and there will likely be further breakthroughs in the future.

Creating virtual reality environments that immerse users in lifelike artificial worlds

As the world's most prominent quantum computing and AI lab's chief scientist, I've been at the forefront of research into new ways for machines to think like humans. I believe quantum computing is one of the most promising avenues for creating genuinely realistic virtual reality environments.

Quantum computers can store and process vast amounts of data orders faster than traditional computers. This makes them ideal for creating virtual environments that are indistinguishable from reality.

One way we can use quantum computers to create lifelike virtual worlds is by using them to generate realistic 3D models of people and objects. Quantum computers can quickly calculate the precise position of every atom in an object, allowing us to create incredibly detailed and accurate 3D models.

Another way quantum computers can be used to create lifelike virtual reality is by simulating entire universes. By running simulations on a quantum computer, we can generate virtual universes that look and feel entirely realistic.

In addition to generating realistic 3D models and simulations, quantum computers can create artificial intelligence indistinguishable from human intelligence. This is because quantum computers can quickly process vast amounts of data, allowing them to learn quickly.

As you can see, quantum computing holds great promise for creating lifelike virtual realities. With quantum computers, we can create virtual worlds indistinguishable from reality. This could have enormous implications for everything from education and training to entertainment and gaming.

Conclusion

The field of artificial intelligence has come a long way in recent years. For example, we have created machine learning algorithms to identify objects, faces, and scenes like humans by developing artificial neural networks and teaching them to recognize human facial expressions. Additionally, by building predictive models of human behavior based on data mining and machine learning techniques, we have created models of human cognition that can be used to guide machine learning. Furthermore, by studying how people use natural language and applying those insights to machine learning, we can design robotic systems that can interact with humans in natural ways.

Looking ahead, there is still much work in artificial intelligence. For example, we need to continue to investigate ways that AI can be used to help people with cognitive impairments or mental health conditions. Additionally, we need to continue to research methods that AI could be used to improve human thinking and decision-making. However, by continued research and development in the field of artificial intelligence, we will be able to overcome these challenges and create even more lifelike and intelligent machines.

www.ingramcontent.com/pod-product-compliance
Lightning Source LLC
LaVergne TN
LVHW051244050326
832903LV00028B/2560